W9-BUU-539

ALL ABOUT ASTHMA

William Ostrow and Vivian Ostrow

Illustrated by Blanche Sims

ALBERT WHITMAN & COMPANY, MORTON GROVE, ILLINOIS

Library of Congress Cataloging-in-Publication Data
Ostrow, William.
All about asthma / William Ostrow and Vivian Ostrow:
illustrated by Blanche Sims.
p. cm.
Summary: The young narrator describes life as an asthmatic,
explaining causes and symptoms of asthma, and discussing ways to
control the disorder to lead a normal life.
ISBN 0-8075-0276-6 (lib. bdg.)
ISBN 0-8075-0275-8 (pbk.)
1. Asthma–Juvenile literature. 2. Asthma in children–Juvenile
literature. [1. Asthma. 2. Children's writings.]
I. Ostrow, Vivian. II. Sims, Blanche, ill. III. Title.
RC591.O77 1989   89-5254
616.2'38–dc19   CIP
                                                           AC

Text © 1989 by William Ostrow and Vivian Ostrow.
Illustrations © 1989 by Blanche Sims.
Published in 1989 by Albert Whitman & Company,
6340 Oakton Street, Morton Grove, Illinois 60053-2723.
Published simultaneously in Canada
by General Publishing, Limited, Toronto.
All rights reserved. Printed in the U.S.A.
10 9 8 7 6 5 4 3

*This book is dedicated
to helping kids with asthma breathe easier.
W.O. & V.O.*

*To George and Voula and Ethel and Michael.
B.S.*

THIS PAGE IS FOR ME TO THANK PEOPLE

My mom—for helping me write this book and for giving me the tendency to sneeze and wheeze.

My dad and brother Alex—for being my dad and brother.

Mrs. Barbara Gould—my third-grade school nurse and friend.

Dr. Ellen Epstein—my allergist and friend. Special thanks for helping me keep all the facts straight in this book.

My grandma—for teaching me about courage.

Garfield—(a cat I'm not allergic to) for helping me keep my sense of humor.

William Ostrow

Contents

Stuck with Asthma   6

What Asthma Is   10

What Asthma Isn't   16

The Asthma Puzzle   20

Help Yourself   23

It's Your Move!   34

Some of the Best People...   36

The Future   40

Stuck with Asthma

My name is William, and I'm stuck with asthma. My story begins around my eighth birthday. First I got a bad cold that turned into pneumonia. While I was at home resting and minding my own business, asthma crept into my life like an evil birthday present.

My first attack was weird. I was sitting and thinking about how I was almost healthy when POW! I couldn't breathe!

After I had coughed and gasped for what seemed like hours (it probably was just a few minutes), my parents took me to the pediatrician. The doctor examined me and said I had asthma. I was so sick and scared that I didn't even put up a fight when he gave me two shots, five minutes apart. My brain couldn't think about anything but how bad I felt, so when the doctor explained what asthma was, I didn't understand a word he said.

On the drive home I was feeling much better, thanks to those shots. I was very tired, and grateful that this asthma thing was over.

Unfortunately, my problems were just beginning.

My asthma got worse very quickly. Soon I was having attacks every few days. I managed to avoid going to the emergency room, but I went to the pediatrician's office so often that when the doctor saw me, *he* got sick.

Without warning, asthma had turned my whole life into a confused mess! I was constantly taking pills and liquids and even puffs from an inhaler that sent medicine from my mouth directly into my lungs, but I never felt safe. Asthma could strike anytime, anyplace. I could be in the middle of a math lesson or a good night's sleep when it came at me out of nowhere. And when an attack began, I never knew whether it would be a half-hour inconvenience or a two-day ordeal.

This is how my asthma attacks felt:

1. My chest would tighten like a gorilla was sitting on it, daring me to take a breath.

2. My breathing would make a strange sound (a wheeze).

3. I would cough a lot as I tried to clear my chest of whatever was blocking the air.

4. My skin would feel sweaty all over.

Even when I felt OK (by now I always had a slight wheeze, but that was beginning to seem normal), I was scared. I didn't know how to avoid attacks or how to help myself when they hit.

My whole family was as confused and frightened as I was. I could hear my folks arguing about the best way to help me while I sat bent over, trying to catch my breath.

What Asthma Is

On one of my many visits, the pediatrician explained what was happening inside me during an attack. He even showed me pictures to make things clearer. Here's what I learned: Normally, when you breathe, air is carried in and out of your lungs by thousands of airways called *bronchioles*. These tubes deliver air to the *alveoli*, the millions of tiny air sacs in the lungs.

Muscles are wrapped all around the bronchioles. Usually these muscles relax when you breathe in. This lets the airways expand, making it easier for air to get into the lungs. When you exhale, the muscles tighten, making the airways more narrow and helping to move the air out. The process repeats itself automatically thousands of times every day, whether you are awake or asleep.

The bronchioles are lined with special cells to produce mucus. This mucus contains something that helps fight infection.

People with asthma have more sensitive bronchioles than other people. They can be allergic to stuff in the air (like dust or pollen) and to foods. They can also be extrasensitive to viral respiratory infections, irritants (like smoke or perfume), exercise, cold air, and stress. All these things are called *triggers* because they can trigger (start) an attack. When an attack begins, two things happen inside the lungs.

1. The muscles wrapped around the bronchioles tighten much more than normal, and the airways stay very narrow. This makes it hard to breathe air in or out.

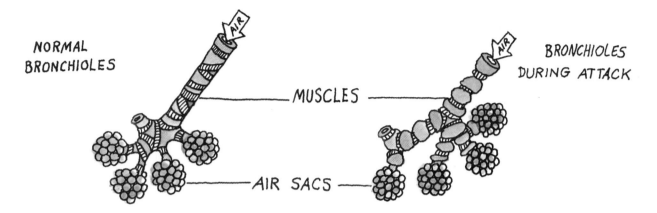

NORMAL BRONCHIOLES

BRONCHIOLES DURING ATTACK

MUSCLES

AIR SACS

2. At the same time, the cells lining the airways swell, and extra mucus is produced. Now the airways are clogged as well as narrow, and it becomes even more difficult to breathe. If you could see inside the airways, they would look like this.

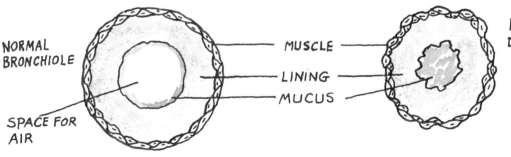

NORMAL BRONCHIOLE

BRONCHIOLE DURING ATTACK

MUSCLE

LINING

MUCUS

SPACE FOR AIR

It is important to remember that this entire process is COMPLETELY REVERSIBLE. The asthma medications you take during an attack (these may be different from any asthma drugs you are taking on a regular basis) act quickly to relax muscles, lessen swelling, and reduce mucus buildup. But the longer you wait to take action during an attack, the smaller the airways become, and the harder it is to open them up again.

This was certainly a lot of information for one wheezing kid to understand, but it was finally starting to make sense.

Now I knew what was happening inside me, but that didn't make living with asthma any easier. I don't know which attacks I hated more—the ones that woke me in the middle of a great dream or the ones that crept up on me during the day.

I do know that when I got attacks at school, I felt scared, helpless, and *embarrassed.* When an attack began, I would try to ignore the whole thing. That usually made my breathing worse. Then it was only a matter of time before I needed to raise my hand and tell the teacher about my problem. Fortunately (for me), Miss Rini, my teacher, had been stuck with asthma as a kid, too. She understood just what I was going through. She would send me to Mrs. Gould, the school nurse.

The nurse's office was my home away from home in third grade. Mrs. Gould was great. Kids who were healthy made up sicknesses just to be near her! She taught me a lot about asthma. She also tried to keep me calm, but those first months were pretty awful.

My medicines (along with instructions) were kept in Mrs. Gould's office. She gave me something for the attack and helped me learn how to time my breathing as I used my inhaler. After I took my medicine, we would talk and wait. Sometimes the attack would go away, but most of the time it just got harder to breathe. Often my mom would have to come and pick me up. Some kids were jealous because I was missing so much school, but I would have given anything to be back in class.

The nurse, my teacher, and my doctor weren't the only people who tried to help. Family and friends kept their eyes open for any and all useful information. My whole family learned from the articles we received. I found out how widespread asthma is from an article my mom's friend Sura sent us. I never would have guessed that over eight million kids have had asthma attacks, and more than two million have it almost all the time (like me). Imagine—over two million kids felt like I did, and I didn't even know one of them (at first)! I learned that asthma is the main reason kids are absent from school. Maybe that's why I wasn't meeting these other kids in the hall—they were all home wheezing! Or maybe they weren't even lucky enough to be at home. I also learned more kids go to emergency rooms or have to stay in hospitals for asthma than for any other chronic illness. (''Chronic'' means you have the disease all the time, or a lot.)

Some facts, like that one about hospitals, weren't very comforting. All I kept thinking was, What did I do to deserve this?

A few articles said that in spite of advances in knowledge and medicines, the number of kids with asthma keeps growing. I wondered why. My doctor said increasing air pollution and better record-keeping (of who has asthma) were partly responsible. He also said that some questions didn't have easy answers. I could see that nothing about asthma was simple or easy!

What Asthma Isn't

Most of this book tells you what asthma is. This chapter is different. It tells what asthma isn't.

1. ASTHMA ISN'T IN YOUR HEAD

It is in your chest, and it's a pain in the neck. Some people (kids, grownups, even a few doctors!) think you give yourself asthma by the way you think. This attitude is annoying and WRONG! Asthma can be made worse by worry and stress, but its underlying cause is *physical*. Even babies a few months old can have asthma, and they are certainly not guilty of "wrong thinking."

2. ASTHMA ISN'T TO BE IGNORED

Even if an attack comes in the middle of something important (like having fun with friends), you can't ignore it. Tell your parent, teacher, nurse, or friend about it, and deal with it. Ignoring attacks makes them worse. If an attack gets out of control, it can be dangerous.

3. ASTHMA ISN'T DOING ANY PERMANENT DAMAGE

The definition of asthma is: a blockage of the airways that is reversible. That means your lungs get congested, and then they become clear again.

4. ASTHMA ISN'T PREDICTABLE

Once you get asthma, it's in your system for life, but no one can tell whether it will bother you often or rarely.

5. ASTHMA ISN'T ANYTHING TO BE ASHAMED OF

Some of the best people (like you and me) have asthma. If you start to wheeze or need to rest or take medicine, don't be embarrassed. Kids sometimes make fun of me because I have asthma, but I found out the less attention I pay them, the sooner they stop. (My real friends never tease me about asthma.) I learned that once you accept your asthma and are comfortable about it, other people will accept it, too.

6. ASTHMA ISN'T YOUR PERSONAL PUNISHMENT FOR ANYTHING BAD YOU'VE DONE

It's been bugging people for over five thousand years. My mother read that even some ancient Egyptian kings (pharaohs) had asthma. The ancient Greeks must have been wheezing also since they came up with the word *asthma*. It is Greek for "panting" (to take short, quick breaths). Of course, knowing this doesn't help you much in the middle of an attack, but it's interesting information when you're feeling fine.

7. ASTHMA ISN'T CATCHING

A friend could be one inch away from me during an attack, and he couldn't catch asthma. It's impossible. (P.S.: You can't get asthma in the mail. That picture on page 6 was a joke.)

8. ASTHMA ISN'T INTERESTED IN YOUR AGE, SEX, INCOME, COLOR, OR WHERE YOU LIVE

All kinds of people everywhere get asthma.

The Asthma Puzzle

Looking for the causes of asthma is like fitting together a huge jigsaw puzzle. To help us find the missing pieces from my asthma puzzle, my parents and I have been working with an allergist. This is a doctor who specializes in treating people with asthma and allergies. There are still a few puzzle parts we don't have, but we certainly know a lot more than we did.

1. Heredity. My allergist said the tendency to have asthma or allergies is inherited. That means you get it from your mom or dad or some other relative. So if your folks have asthma or allergies (my mom has both), you could develop these conditions, too. For some kids (like me), allergies can trigger asthma attacks. Ordinary things like furry cats that don't bother most people can make me sneeze, wheeze, and gasp for breath.

Looking back, I realize the pneumonia set off my first asthma attack, but I was born with the *tendency* to be allergic and asthmatic (thanks, Mom). It was good to discover the heredity piece of my asthma puzzle, even though finding it didn't cure anything.

2. Triggers. Since some of my attacks are triggered by allergies, a *scratch test* gave me a lot of important puzzle pieces. First, the allergist drew lines on my arm. Then she placed extracts of tree, grass, and ragweed pollen, dander, mold, feathers, and dust on my skin near each line and scratched the top skin layer. After about fifteen minutes, she checked to see which areas were red, swollen, and itchy. If an area was red and swollen, we'd know I was allergic to what she'd put there. (This scratch test doesn't hurt; I just got a little itchy.)

Many other things can trigger an attack in a sensitive person. These common triggers include aspirin, perfume, smoke, exhaust fumes (from cars), viral respiratory infections, cold air, and exercise. (This doesn't mean you cannot exercise. It just means you have to be careful. I will talk more about exercise later in the book.)

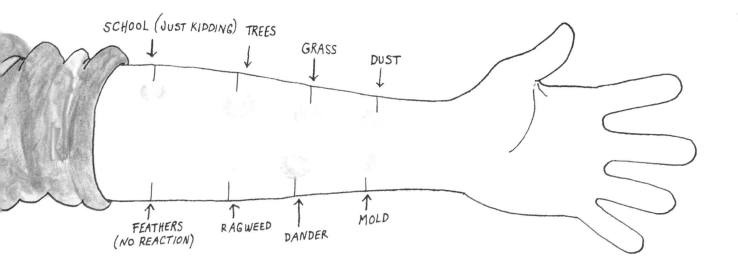

Laughing, crying, yelling, and stress can also cause an asthma attack. In fact, laughter is one of my most annoying triggers. There I am with my brother Alex, laughing hysterically about something, when I start coughing and gasping for air. Mom says I ought to be alert so I can stop laughing in time, but it's so much fun to crack up like that! Oh, well, I guess she's right. Asthma is no laughing matter for me.

3. Diary Clues. To find out more about what causes *your* attacks, you (or your parents) should keep a diary. Write down foods you've eaten, weather, activities, any sickness, and, of course, asthma attacks. In just a few months you'll be getting puzzle pieces even the best doctor couldn't give you. My diary showed that every time I ate hot dogs, I got an attack. I miss hot dogs, but I certainly don't miss those attacks!

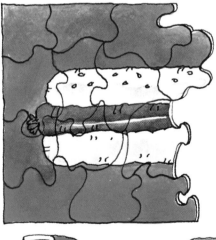

No matter how much you know or how well you keep track of things, you won't be able to find a cause for every attack. Asthma is very tricky. Sometimes a trigger will cause an attack immediately, and sometimes there is a delay that can range from hours to a day or so. You can learn enough to avoid most of your triggers. Then coping with attacks you can't escape isn't such a big job.

Help Yourself

There is a lot you can do to avoid asthma attacks and to make them less severe when you do get stuck with one. In the team of doctor, parents, and kid, *you* are the key player.

1. Find Dr. Right. Asthma is complicated! The worse your asthma is, the more difficult it will be to control. That's why when you have your first attack, *you should go to the doctor as soon as you can.* It is also important to make sure you go to the *right* doctor. When my pediatrician couldn't stop my asthma from getting worse, he sent me to an allergist. The allergist asked me questions and ran tests to find out what triggered my attacks.

I've found from personal experience that a good doctor *listens* carefully, *cares* about his or her patients, and *knows* how to help them. The best way for you and your parents to judge if you're going to the right doctor is to see how your asthma is doing. No doctor has a miracle cure, but if after a while you're getting worse instead of better, you need to search for Dr. Right.

2. Participate. Of course, the best doctor in the world can't help unless you and your parents do your part. You must (along with your parents) *observe* (a diary aids your memory); *communicate* (don't keep secrets—the doctor learns how you're doing from *you*); and *cooperate.*

It isn't always easy to follow the doctor's suggestions (give up a pet, dust-proof a bedroom), but I know I can breathe a lot easier now than when I had a furry cat running around my cluttered bedroom.

3. Take Your Medicine. Since everyone's asthma is different, your doctor will decide with you what *you* need. IT IS UP TO YOU TO UNDERSTAND WHEN AND HOW TO TAKE YOUR MEDICINE. Even though taking medicine gets to be a drag sometimes, especially when you're busy at school or having fun, it's very important.

You might need to take many medicines every day (like I do) or just one, once in a while. My daily medicine schedule was reached after months of trial and error. Each day I take six pills (two different medicines); inhale fourteen puffs (two other medicines) into my mouth; and breathe two sniffs from my nasal inhaler. If I get a bad attack, I can take two more medicines—which makes a total of seven! This schedule changes sometimes depending on the season and on how well my asthma is being managed. The goal is to control my asthma using the least amount of drugs.

Keep in mind that medicines can have side effects (do extra things you weren't expecting). You should always tell your parents and your doctor about anything strange or different in the way you feel.

Your doctor may recommend a peak-flow meter. With it, you can monitor your breathing and take early action against an attack.

Sometimes even catching an attack early and taking extra medicine are not enough. When you've done everything you can and your attack is not going away, *call the doctor.* You may need special medications that only the doctor has. But the more you know and the better managed your asthma is, the less often this will happen. I haven't gone to the doctor's office because of an attack for over a year. I never miss being the "lucky" kid who left school to rush to the doctor!

4. Avoid Triggers. Here are some of my triggers:

Dander—It comes from animal hair. Because of asthma I had to give up my lovable black cat, Fasta. Just thinking about it makes me mad and sad.

Cold Air—On cold, windy days, I wear a ski mask that covers my nose and mouth so I can breathe warm air.

Dust—I used to have a nice, messy room full of books, toys, and anything else I could find. Now that I know I'm allergic to dust, I have a nice, clean room with an air purifier in the middle of it. Lucky me! I really *can* play with my things—I just have to remember to put them away so they don't collect dust.

Foods—Foods to check out first as possible triggers are milk, eggs, nuts, and chocolate. Certain foods are off limits for me. Some I miss (like chocolate); some I don't (like peas). I still pig out on what I can eat!

Smoke—It is bad for me, and everyone else on the planet.

5. Take Allergy Shots. My scratch tests showed that I am allergic to many things in the air (mold, dust, all kinds of pollen). Knowing this left me some confusing choices. I could wear a protective spacesuit, or I could spend my summers indoors in air conditioning (which filters out most of my triggers) and my winters who knows where? But then I'd miss all the fun of summer, and my folks would probably miss me in the winter! Instead, I get allergy shots for dust, grass and tree pollen, mold, and some other triggers I can't even remember.

The shots hardly hurt, and I got used to them quickly. They contain small amounts of the things I am allergic to so my system can get accustomed to them a little bit at a time. I know it sounds weird to inject things into your body that your body doesn't like to begin with, but I'm breathing easier now, thanks to those shots.

Allergy shots aren't perfect. For instance, they don't start working right away, and it's a nuisance to get them every week or two weeks or each month. Shots may not help everyone. Some people who have asthma don't have allergies. Ask your doctor if shots might work for you. For me, until something better comes along, I'd rather get shots than hide from the air.

6. Relax. Relaxing helps you get through an attack, but when it's hard to breathe, it's hard to relax! Sometimes deep breathing (in through the nose, out through the mouth) is all you need to escape a mild attack. My friend Marsha taught me that when I feel an attack coming, I should imagine myself in my favorite place, South Carolina, riding the waves and having a great time. This puts me in a very peaceful mood, and my asthma floats away with the tide (sometimes). Reading, listening to music, playing my piano, violin, or drums, and molding clay are other ways to ease asthma out of my life.

The more I know about my asthma and what I can do to help myself, the more relaxed I can be during an attack. I hope this book will teach you a lot about your asthma so you can relax, too. Of course, sometimes you need to do more than relax, but it's always worth trying because it's fun and there are never any bad side effects.

7. Drink. The school nurse told me to drink at the first sign of an attack. Later, I learned that liquids help keep my airways moist, loosening the mucus that has built up. You can drink water, juices, or whatever you like. My allergist told me to avoid drinks with caffeine because some of my asthma medicines speed my heartbeat, and so does caffeine. (A rapid heartbeat is an example of a side effect that is acceptable, but shouldn't be made worse.) At the first sign of an attack, drink to your health!

8. Exercise. (My definition: playing and having fun while in motion.) If you think exercise is another trigger to be avoided, think again! Most doctors agree that it helps kids with asthma.

Exercise can trigger an asthma attack, but this doesn't mean that *no* exercise is good. Exercise keeps fighters in shape for their fights, and it keeps our bodies in shape for our bouts with asthma. My allergist told me that regular exercise strengthens your whole body, improves the way your lungs work, and helps your system use oxygen more efficiently. If you exercise regularly, you are *less* likely to get exercise-triggered asthma, and your body will be more able to tolerate the strain of shortness of breath. Everybody, but especially kids with asthma, should warm up (start slowly) before exercise and cool down (stop gradually) afterward. While exercising, breathe in through your nose. This warms the air before it reaches your lungs.

I'm not a great athlete, but I can see the connection between exercise and feeling better in my own life. Summer is always my healthiest season. I spend a lot of time at the beach, and since there are no trees, grasses, molds, pets, smoke, or dust around, it makes sense that I feel pretty good. There is something else that makes summer such a happy, healthy time. I swim all summer. I don't do any special routines. I just have fun, and while I'm doing it I get lots of exercise.

My allergist told me that swimming is great for kids with asthma because it exercises the whole body and increases breathing abilities. Since it's often done in a warm, humid atmosphere, it can help moisten the airways.

If you're not into swimming, then basketball, softball, and volleyball are great, too! Sports like running may be too exhausting for some people but fine for others. Whatever you decide, first talk to your doctor about it. Be sure to ask if you need to take any special medications before activities (I do). Pick something you like to do, and start

slowly—let's say ten minutes of biking a day. I bet you'll be surprised to see that you can build your body up, slow asthma down, and have fun all at the same time!

9. Go to an Asthma Conference. A while ago my family went to an asthma conference at a local hospital. (It was actually one meeting each week for five weeks.) The parents listened to various doctors speak about asthma. After the talks they could ask questions. The kids went into a big gymlike room. There we made friends, learned about karate, practiced relaxed breathing, and had a great time. If there is something like this in your neighborhood, I think you should go to it. Like me, you will probably learn about asthma and have fun, too.

At the conference, I got to compare notes with many boys and girls who have asthma. When I met kids who were really scared because their asthma was out of control, I thought about how much better things had gotten for me. I knew how to avoid many of my triggers, and when asthma did catch up to me, I could usually deal with it successfully. I felt like the weight of my asthma had become much lighter.

I told my parents how I felt, and they were quick to agree. I got the feeling that between us, we could now handle whatever asthma threw our way. Those first few months of worry and confusion were behind us, and the whole family was more at peace.

It's Your Move!

I belong to many clubs and organizations. Some (like fencing and Scouting), I can only participate in when my asthma isn't bothering me. Others, like Student Council and Newspaper Club, I can usually do because I don't have to be too active. One of my favorite groups is Chess Club. I've been playing chess for years. I like chess because it makes me think and plot, usually against someone older, and I like a challenge.

One day it occurred to me that having asthma was kind of like playing chess.

IT'S ME AGAINST THE FORCES OF ASTHMA

1. I've got to know my opponent. (Now I do.)

2. I try to outwit him at first. (Taking my daily medicine and allergy shots helps protect me from asthma.)

3. If he mounts an attack, I know what countermoves to make. (I relax, drink liquids, and take extra medicine if necessary.)

4. I have strategies mapped out to keep one jump ahead of him. (Avoiding my triggers keeps me in safe territory.)

5. No matter what, I've got to KEEP MY GUARD UP and keep thinking, because if I don't, ASTHMA WINS!

Some of the Best People...

I can remember sitting in the nurse's office last year while all the other kids were in class. I felt like I was the only kid on the planet who had asthma.

As people found out about my asthma, I learned I was not alone. The girl next door (now fifteen) had it worse than I do (it hardly seems possible). Now she is on the track team, with her eyes set on the Olympics. Honest! A girl around the corner (she is about five) is also doing much better this year than she did before. A grown woman my mom knows just got asthma a year ago. A man a few blocks away has had it since he was a kid.

As I told you, my mom has it, but it rarely bothers her. My Uncle Barry, who is a doctor, had it when he was young, but it never annoys him anymore. One day at the allergist's office, I saw a police officer, and I asked the doctor if the officer had asthma. She said yes. She also told me that Benjamin Ward, the head of all the policemen in New York City (TOP COP), has asthma. That really surprised me!!

During a family get-together, my cousin Dan told me that Teddy Roosevelt had asthma as a kid. This was exciting news, and I needed to investigate it further. I went to the library and took out every book I saw about Teddy Roosevelt.

I learned that when Teddy was my age, his asthma was so bad that he couldn't even go to school. To someone without asthma, this might sound like fun, but we know being home coughing and wheezing is no vacation! Way back then (the 1860s), doctors didn't know much about treating asthma.

When I read about Teddy Roosevelt, I felt like I was reading about myself. He wanted to be a doctor (so do I), he needed glasses (I need them to see the blackboard), he loved nature and collecting weird stuff (me, too), and of course there's the asthma. It amazed me that from being such a sick kid he became one of the most famous, powerful presidents of all time. As I read I found myself taking deeper breaths. Just like Teddy Roosevelt, I could do and be anything!

Besides Benjamin Ward and Teddy Roosevelt, I've learned about many other famous people with asthma: former Steeler running back Rocky Bleier; Olympic star Jackie Joyner-Kersee (named "World's Best Female Athlete" at the 1988 Olympics); actresses Helen Hayes and Elizabeth Taylor and singer-dancer-actress Liza Minnelli; Jim "Catfish" Hunter, who pitched for the New York Yankees, my favorite team; former vice-president Walter Mondale; singer Wayne Newton; Joseph Pulitzer, publisher and founder of the Pulitzer Prize; Christopher Reeve (alias Superman); writer-comedian Carl Reiner and comedian Don Rickles; and movie director Martin Scorsese.

It's a pretty impressive list, but remember, I told you that some of the best people (like us) have asthma.

Just like all the people on the list, I will always have asthma, but the odds are good that it will bother me less as I get older. I'm told many kids find their asthma grows milder by the time they leave their teens. If I'm lucky, like my mom and uncle, maybe I will rarely have to think about it. I certainly hope that happens, but I'm not holding my breath (ha, ha, ha). I know I have to live with asthma now, so I might as well make the best of it.

I still sit in the nurse's office sometimes waiting for an attack to go away, but now I don't feel so alone.

The Future

There is no cure for asthma (yet). Maybe someday you or I will make the great discovery that will make this ancient sickness disappear. For now, it's good to know that scientists are learning more about asthma and its treatment every year. Three of the drugs I take weren't even around a short while ago.

Thanks to good doctors and new medicines, kids like you and me can do just about anything we want to. For me, the key to successfully managing my asthma was learning as much about it as I could. I hope this book helps you to learn so you can understand and cope with your asthma better.

When I got stuck with asthma, more than anything else I wanted to talk to another kid who had the same problem I did. I felt sure if I could find such a kid, my asthma would be a lot easier to live with. If you feel that way, too, I'd be happy to hear from you. Please enclose a stamped, self-addressed envelope. I promise to write back.

William

William Ostrow
P.O. Box 275
Island Park, N.Y. 11558